To _____

From _____

Date _____

365 Things Every Teacher Should Know

© 2005 Christian Art Gifts, RSA
    Christian Art Gifts Inc., IL, USA

First edition © 2005
Second edition © 2010

Compiled by Wilma le Roux and Monica Schaller

Designed by Christian Art Gifts
Images used under license from Shutterstock.com

Printed in China

ISBN 978-1-77036-558-2

11 12 13 14 15 16 17 18 19 20 – 12 11 10 9 8 7 6 5 4 3

365

things every
Teacher
should know

christian
art gifts®

Contents

Foreword

Enjoy the 365 pearls of wisdom specially gathered to uplift and sustain you and to bring the occasional smile after a long day.

The greatest Teacher of all time, Jesus Christ, is the source of all knowledge and wisdom. May the treasured words from Scripture provide added strength and inspiration as you fulfill the duties of your very special calling.

The Child

1.

To bring a child up in the way he should go, travel that way yourself once in a while.

Josh Billings

2.

How soon do we forget
what elders used to know:
That children should be raised,
not left like weeds to grow.

Art Buck

3.

A child is owed the greatest respect;
if ever you have something disgraceful in
mind, don't ignore your son's tender years.

Juvenal

4.

Go practice if you will with men
and women: leave the child alone
for Christ's particular love's sake.

Robert Browning

5.

Children cannot be made good
by making them happy, but they can be
made happy by making them good.

E. J. Kiefer

6.

Children have never been very good
at listening to their elders, but they
have never failed to imitate them.

James Baldwin

7.

A child's life is like a piece of paper
on which every passerby leaves a mark.

Chinese Proverb

8.

Upon our children – how they
are taught – rests the fate – or
fortune – of tomorrow's world.

B. C. Forbes

9.

The whining schoolboy,
with his satchel,
and shining morning face,
creeping like a snail
unwillingly to school.

William Shakespeare

10.

Nothing you do for children is ever wasted.
They seem not to notice us, hovering,
averting our eyes, and they seldom offer
thanks, but what we do is never wasted.

Garrison Kellor

11.

The conscience of children is formed
by the influences that surround them;
their notions of good and evil are a result
of the moral atmosphere they breathe.

Jean Paul Richter

12.

Children are like wet
cement. Whatever falls on
them leaves an impression.

Haim Ginott

13.

If a child lives with love,
he learns that the world is
a wonderful place to live in.

14.

Pretty much all the honest truth telling
there is in the world is done by children.

Oliver Wendell Holmes

15.

Teenagers are the vanguard
of tomorrow. They are a fresh
breeze in a stale world.

Dan Valentine

16.

Children are not things to be
molded, but people to be unfolded.

Jess Lair

17.

To grown people a girl of fifteen
and a half is a child still; to herself
she is very old and very real – more
real, perhaps, than ever before or after.

Margaret Widdemer

18.

You can learn many things
from children. How much
patience you have, for instance.

Franklin P. Jones

19.

Teenagers are people
who express a burning
desire to be different
by dressing exactly alike.

20.

A child is not a vase to be
filled, but a fire to be lit.

Francois Rabelais

21.

Since teenagers are too old to do the
things kids do and not old enough
to do the things adults do,
they do things nobody else does.

22.

A child becomes an adult when he
realizes that he has a right not only
to be right, but also to be wrong.

Thomas Szasz

23.

Childhood is not from birth to a certain
age and at a certain age the child is
grown and puts away childish things.
Childhood is the kingdom where nobody
dies – nobody that matters, that is.

Edna St. Vincent Millay

24.

The childhood shows the man
as morning shows the day.

John Milton

25.

There is always one moment
in childhood when the door
opens and lets the future in.

Graham Greene

26.

There is no such whetstone to
sharpen a good wit and encourage
a will to learning, as is praise.

Roger Ascham

27.

Each human mind is a galaxy
of intelligences, wherein
shines the light of a billion stars.

Timothy Ferries

28.

A child is a person who is going
to carry on what you have started ...
the fate of humanity is in his hands.

Abraham Lincoln

29.

Learning is either
ongoing or it is nothing.

Frank Tyger

30.

Teach me knowledge and
good judgment, for I
believe in your commands.

Psalm 119:66

31.

A child is an island of curiosity
surrounded by a sea of question marks.

32.

Badgered, snubbed and scolded on the
one hand; petted, flattered and indulged on
the other – it is astonishing how many children
work their way up to an honest manhood in
spite of parents and friends. Human nature
has an element of great toughness in it.

Henry Ward Beecher

33.

Tell me, and I forget, teach
me, and I may remember,
involve me, and I learn.

Benjamin Franklin

34.

Almost every child would learn to
write sooner if he were allowed to
do his homework in wet cement.

35.

You can teach a student a lesson for
a day; but if you teach him to learn
by creating curiosity, he will continue
the learning process as long as he lives.

Clay P. Bedford

36.

"A student is not above his teacher,
nor a servant above his master. It is
enough for the student to be like his
teacher, and the servant like his master."

Matthew 10:24-25

37.

Every child is born with a great capacity
for knowledge ... The purpose of the
teacher is to "draw out", not to "cram in".
We must create interest in the heart and mind
of the child that will make him reach out and
take hold upon the things he is taught.

Henrietta C. Mears

38.

It is not what is poured
into the student, but what
is planted, that counts.

Eugene P. Berten

39.

The child becomes largely what it
is taught, hence we must watch what
we teach it, and how we live before it.

Timothy Ferries

40.

There are not seven wonders
of the world in the eyes of a
child. There are seven million.

Walt Streightiff

41.

It's what you learn after
you know it all that counts.

John Wooden

42.

Words of praise, indeed, are almost
as necessary to warm a child into
congenial life as acts of kindness
and affection. Judicious praise is
to children what sun is to flowers.

Christian Bovée

43.

If a child lives with praise,
he learns to be appreciative.

44.

Minds are like parachutes.
They only work when open.

45.

The best compliment to a child or friend is
the feeling you give him that he has been
set free to make his own enquiries, to come
to conclusions that are right for him,
whether or not they coincide with your own.

Alistair Cooke

46.

We are apt to forget that
children watch examples better
than they listen to preaching.

Roy L. Smith

47.

As we look to the future we realize that the child is the key to peace. How he grows, the personality he develops, the attitude he acquires, the knowledge and the experience he has – all determine how successfully he will live with others in this rapidly shrinking world.

Lydia Ann Lynde

48.

The possibilities of any child are the most intriguing and stimulating in all creation.

Ray L. Wilbur

49.

Children's games are hardly games. Children are never more serious than when they play.

Michel de Montaigne

Teachers
and Teaching

50.

A teacher affects eternity; he can
never tell where his influence stops.

Henry Brooks Adams

51.

Blessed is the hand that prepares
a pleasure for a child, for there is no
saying when and where it may bloom forth.

Douglas William Jerrold

52.

My joy in learning is partly
that it enables me to teach.

Seneca

53.

Even while they teach, men learn.

Seneca

54.

A schoolmaster should have an
atmosphere of awe, and walk wonderingly,
as if he was amazed at being himself.

Walter Bagehot

55.

Life is amazing and the teacher
better prepare himself to be
the medium for that amazement.

Edward Blishen

56.

One good teacher in a lifetime may sometimes
change a delinquent into a solid citizen.

Philip Wylie

57.

The best teacher is the one who suggests
rather than dogmatizes, and inspires the
listener with the wish to teach himself.

Edward Bulwer-Lytton

58.

The best teacher is one who ...
kindles an inner fire, arouses moral
enthusiasm, inspires the student
with a vision of what he may become,
and reveals the worth and permanency
of moral and spiritual and cultural values.

Harold Garnett

59.

The whole art of teaching is on the art of
awakening the natural curiosity of young
minds for the purpose of satisfying it afterwards.

Anatole France

60.

To teach, to guide,
to explain, to help, to nurture –
these are life's noblest attainments.

Frank Tyger

61.

To teach is to learn twice.

Joseph Joubert

62.

The teacher who is attempting to teach
without inspiring the pupil with a
desire to learn is hammering on cold iron.

Horace Mann

63.

A great teacher is not simply one who
imparts knowledge to his students, but
one who awakens their interest in it and
makes them eager to pursue it for themselves.
He is a spark plug, not a fuel pipe.

M. J. Berrill

64.

You, then, who teach others,
do you not teach yourself?

Romans 2:21

65.

No mechanical device can replace the
teacher. Thus far, no substitute has been
found for the impact of mind upon mind.
Personality upon personality. Teachers may
overcome limitations in environment, but
they themselves are absolutely essential.

Eleanor L. Doan

66.

Old teachers never die,
they just grade away!

Bob Phillips

67.

If I have the gift of prophecy and can
fathom all mysteries and all knowledge,
and if I have a faith that can move
mountains, but have not love, I am nothing.

1 Corinthians 13:2

68.

The educator becomes God's
mind at work to help grow the best
possible plants in God's garden.
He exists to prepare the soil,
to sow the good seed, to weed,
to water, and to harvest.

Nels F. S. Ferre

69.

A great teacher has always been
measured by the number of
students who have surpassed him.

Don Robinson

70.

Enthusiasm is like
having two right hands.

Elbert Hubbard

71.

Teachers can be found after school –
taking aspirin, washing blackboards,
rehearsing plays, sewing costumes for
Christmas pageants – and just sitting at
a desk waiting for the strength to go home.

Dan Valentine

72.

When asked what subject she taught,
she answered that she did not
teach subjects – she taught children!

73.

The mediocre teacher tells.
The good teacher explains.
The superior teacher demonstrates.
The great teacher inspires.

William Arthur Ward

74.

Most of all, a teacher is somebody who
likes somebody else's children – and has
the strength left to go to the PTA meeting.

75.

The task of the modern educator
is not to cut down jungles,
but to irrigate deserts.

C. S. Lewis

76.

Good teachers are those
who are able to inspire young
minds without losing their own.

77.

An important personal quality for
a teacher is that he cares about humanity.
If he doesn't, he is taking his pay illegally.

Edward C. Helwick

78.

Teachers should be held in highest honor.
They are the allies of the legislators; they
have agency on the prevention of crime;
they aid in regulating the atmosphere,
whose incessant action and pressure cause
the life-blood to circulate, and to return pure
and healthful to the heart of the nation.

Lydia Sigourney

79.

The true aim of everyone who aspires
to be a teacher should be not to impart
his own opinions, but to kindle minds.

Frederick W. Robertson

80.

There's nothing that can help you
understand your beliefs more than trying
to explain them to an inquisitive child.

Frank A. Clark

81.

In teaching you cannot see the fruit
of a day's work. It is invisible and
remains so, maybe for twenty years.

Jacques Barzun

82.

What nobler employment ...
than that of instructing
the younger generation.

Cicero

83.

I touch the future: I teach.

Christa McAuliffe

84.

Our greatest obligation to our children is to prepare them to understand and deal effectively with the world in which they live and not the world we have known or the world we prefer to have.

Grayson Kirk

85.

Teaching is not a lost art, but the regard for it is a lost tradition.

Jacques Barzun

86.

When our children
run to school and walk from school,
I will know that our teachers
are fulfilling their sacred mission well.

J. A. Rosenkrantz

87.

You teach little by what you say.
You teach most by what you are.

Henrietta C. Mears

88.

Teaching kids to count is fine.
But teaching them what counts is best.

Bob Talbert

89.

Good teaching is one-fourth
preparation and three-fourths theater.

Gail Godwin

90.

Never undertake anything for
which you wouldn't have the courage
to ask the blessings of heaven.

Georg Christoph Lichtenberg

91.

You are never defeated as long as
you don't think the job is impossible.

Dale Carnegie

92.

The art of teaching is
the art of assisting discovery.

Mark van Doren

93.

The first step
toward success
in any occupation
is to become interested in it.

William Osler

94.

To know when one's self
is interested, is the first condition
of interesting other people.

John Morley

95.

The test of a vocation is the
love of the drudgery it involves.

Logan Pearsall Smith

96.

Think not of yourself as the architect
of your career but as the sculptor.
Expect to have to do a lot of hard hammering
and chiseling and scraping and polishing.

B. C. Forbes

97.

The goodness that thou
mayest do this day, do it;
delay it not until tomorrow.

Geoffrey Chaucer

98.

Kindness is a language the deaf can hear and the dumb can understand.

99.

Be sincere. Be simple in words, manners and gestures. Amuse as well as instruct. If you can make a man laugh, you can make him think and make him like and believe you.

Alfred E. Smith

100.

Each morning sees a task begun, each evening sees it close; something attempted, something done has earned a night's repose.

Henry Wadsworth Longfellow

101.

The confidence that we have in
ourselves gives birth to much
of that which we have in others.

Francois de la Rochefoucauld

102.

He has achieved success who has
loved much, laughed often and
been an inspiration to little children.

103.

He who helps a child helps humanity
with an immediateness which no
other help given to human creatures
in any other stage of human
life can possibly give again.

Phillips Brooks

104.

Never discourage anyone
who continually makes progress,
no matter how slow.

105.

It's the less bright students
who make teachers teach better.

Malcolm Forbes

106.

"Take My yoke upon you and learn from
Me, for I am gentle and humble in heart."

Matthew 11:29

107.

There is nothing more inspiring than having
a mind unfold before you. Let people who
teach have a calling. It is never just a job.

Abraham Kaplan

108.

I care not what subject is being
taught if only it is taught well.

Thomas H. Huxley

109.

No bubble is so iridescent or
floats longer than that blown
by the successful teacher.

Sir William Osler

110.

Teach people as if they were what
they ought to be and you help them
become what they are capable of being.

Johann Wolfgang von Goethe

111.

The teaching of Christ is more
excellent than all the advice of
the saints, and he who has His
Spirit will find in it a hidden manna.

Thomas à Kempis

112.

In a society safe and worthy to
be free, teaching which produces
a willingness to lead, as well as a
willingness to follow, must be given to all.

William F. Russell

Knowledge and Education

113.

Never mistake knowledge for wisdom.
One helps you make a living and the
other helps you make a life.

Sandra Carey

114.

The fear of the LORD is the
beginning of knowledge.

Proverbs 1:7

115.

Knowledge is free at the library.
Just bring your own container.

116.

Knowledge is a comfortable and necessary
retreat and shelter for us in an advanced
age; and if we do not plant it while young;
it will give us no shade when we grow old.

Lord Chesterfield

117.

Real knowledge, like everything else of the highest value, is not to be obtained easily. It must be worked for, studied for, thought for, and, more than all, it must be prayed for.

Thomas Arnold

118.

Knowledge is the small part of ignorance that we arrange and classify.

Ambrose Bierce

119.

Knowledge is a treasure but practice is the key to it.

Thomas Fuller

120.

Every branch of knowledge which a good man possesses, he may apply to some good purpose.

Claudius Buchanan

121.

What a man knows should find expression in what he does. The chief value of superior knowledge is that it leads to a performing manhood.

Christian Bovée

122.

Knowledge is love and light and vision.

Helen Keller

123.

If a man empties his purse into
his head, no one can take it away
from him. An investment in
knowledge always pays the best interest.

Benjamin Franklin

124.

Learning is acquired by reading
books; but much more necessary
than learning, the knowledge of the
world, is only to be acquired by reading men,
and studying all the various editions of them.

Lord Chesterfield

125.

The thing is, in this life you can
know a great deal about
something and still be wrong.

Sir Len Hutton

126.

Knowledge always desires increase;
it is like fire, which must first be
kindled by some external agent, but
which will afterwards propagate itself.

Samuel Johnson

127.

It is not so important to know
everything as to know the exact
value of everything to appreciate what
we learn and to arrange what we know.

Hannah Moore

128.

Knowledge is the only
instrument of production that is
not subject to diminishing returns.

J. M. Clark

129.

If you have knowledge,
let others light their candles at it.

Margaret Fuller

130.

And if you call out for insight and cry
aloud for understanding, and if you
look for it as for silver and search for
it as for hidden treasure, then you
will understand the fear of the
LORD and find the knowledge of God.

Proverbs 2:3-5

131.

We cannot hold a torch
to light another's path
without brightening our own.

Ben Sweetland

132.

There are two ways of spreading light: to
be the candle or the mirror that reflects it.

Edith Wharton

133.

The larger the island of knowledge
the longer the shoreline of wonder.

Ralph W. Stockman

134.

Knowledge is happiness, because
to have knowledge – broad, deep
knowledge – is to know true ends
from false, and lofty things from low.

Helen Keller

135.

Education is the defense of the nations.

Edmund Burke

136.

When I was young I was sure of everything; in
a few years, having been mistaken a thousand
times, I was not half so sure of most things as
I was before; at present, I am hardly sure of
anything but what God has revealed to me.

John Wesley

137.

Knowledge is not the most important
thing in the world. Love is essential.

Francois de Fénelon

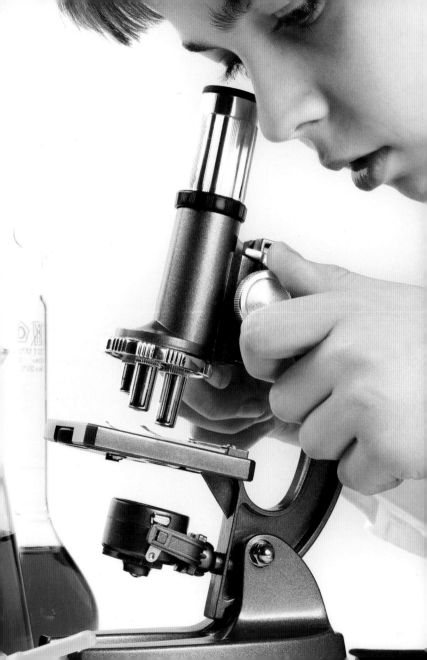

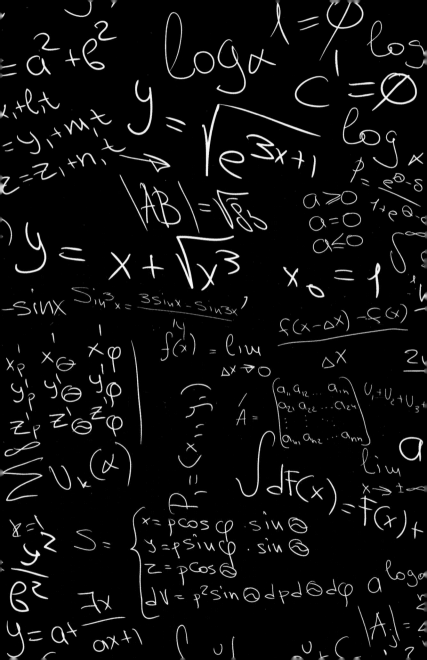

138.

Beware that you are not
swallowed up in books. One ounce of
love is worth a pound of knowledge.

John Wesley

139.

'Tis education forms the common mind,
just as the twig is bent, the tree's inclined.

Alexander Pope

140.

Education has for its object
the formation of character.

Herbert Spencer

141.

The aim of education is the
knowledge not of facts but of values.

William Ralph Inge

142.

Education is what survives when what
has been learned has been forgotten.

B. F. Skinner

143.

The man who knows not and knows
that he knows not is a child – teach him.

Arabian Proverb

144.

All education is continuous dialogue –
question and answer that pursue
every problem to the horizon.

William O. Douglas

145.

One of the chief objects of education
should be to widen the windows
through which we view the world.

Arnold Glasgow

146.

The two basic processes of
education are knowing and valuing.

Robert J. Havighurst

147.

Our world is a college, events are teachers,
happiness is the diploma God gives man.

Newell Dwight Hillis

148.

My idea of education is to unsettle the minds
of the young and inflame their intellects.

Robert M. Hutchins

149.

An educated man is one on whom nothing is lost.

Wendell Smith

150.

The aim of education should be to convert the
mind into a living fountain, and not a reservoir.
That which is filled by merely pumping in,
will be emptied by pumping out.

John H. Mason

151.

Just as education without humanity
is the most dangerous thing in the world,
so education with love, human understanding
and cooperation is the greatest hope of the world.

Joy Elmer Morgan

152.

The future of civilization is, to a great extent,
being written in the classrooms of the world.

Milton L. Smith

153.

The real object of education is to give
children resources that will endure as
long as life endures; habits that time will
ameliorate, not destroy; occupation that will
render sickness tolerable, solitude pleasant,
age venerable, life more dignified and useful.

Sydney Smit

154.

The great aim of education
is not knowledge but action.

Herbert Spencer

155.

School is a building that has
four walls – with tomorrow inside.

Lon Watters

156.

The test and use of man's
education is that he finds pleasure
in the exercise of his mind.

Jacques Barzun

157.

Books are the compass and telescopes
and sextants and charts which other
men have prepared to help us navigate
the dangerous seas of human life.

Jesse Lee Bennet

158.

Education's purpose is to replace
an empty mind with an open one.

Malcolm S. Forbes

159.

"Therefore every teacher of the
law who has been instructed about
the kingdom of heaven is like the owner
of a house who brings out of his
storeroom new treasures as well as old."

Matthew 13:52

160.

The main part of intellectual education
is not the acquisition of facts
but learning how to make facts live.

Oliver Wendell Holmes

161.

Education without God is
like a ship without a compass.

162.

Books are lighthouses erected
in the great sea of time.

E. P. Whipple

163.

All that mankind has done, thought,
gained or been: it is lying in magic
preservation in the pages of books.

Thomas Carlyle

164.

A good book is the precious lifeblood
of a master spirit, embalmed and
treasured up on purpose to life beyond life.

John Milton

165.

Book: A garden carried in a pocket.

Arabian Proverb

166.

We take up a book at one time, and
see nothing in it; at another, it is full of
weighty remarks and precious thoughts.

Cardinal John Henry Newman

167.

A book is a garden, an orchard,
a storehouse, a party,
a company by the way, a counselor,
a multitude of counselors.

Henry Ward Beecher

168.

If minds are truly alive they will seek
out books, for books are the human race
recounting its memorable experiences,
confronting its problems, searching for
solutions, drawing the blueprints for
its futures. To read books is one way of
growing along with one's fellows-in-growth.

Harry A. Overstreet

169.

Books are ships that pass
through the vast seas of time.

Francis Bacon

170.

The true university of these
days is a collection of books.

Thomas Carlyle

Discipline

171.

Only the man who can impose
discipline upon himself is fit to discipline
others or can impose discipline on others.

William Feather

172.

Re raising children: Love
without discipline, isn't.

Malcolm Forbes

173.

To build is often a slow and difficult
task stretching over years. To destroy
can be the thoughtless action of one day.

Winston Churchill

174.

Every time you lose your
temper you advertise yourself.

175.

Rudeness, yelling, anger, and swearing
are a weak man's imitation of strength.

176.

Love of God and love of the brethren
are the true preparation and discipline for life.

Bernard C. Newman

177.

No life ever grows great until it
is focused, dedicated, disciplined.

Harry Emerson Fosdick

178.

Discipline without freedom is tyranny.
Freedom without discipline is chaos.

Cullen Hightower

179.

Behavior is the mirror in which
everyone shows their image.

180.

Be dogmatically true,
obstinately holy,
immovably honest,
desperately kind,
fixedly upright.

Charles H. Spurgeon

181.

No discipline seems pleasant at the time,
but painful. Later on, however, it
produces a harvest of righteousness and
peace for those who have been trained by it.

Hebrews 12:11

182.

If you are patient in one moment
of anger, you will escape
a hundred days of sorrow.

Chinese Proverb

183.

Act nothing in furious passion.
It's putting to sea in a storm.

Thomas Fuller

184.

A show of temper is never a hit.

Frank Tyger

185.

Every stroke our fury strikes
is sure to hit ourselves at last.

William Penn

186.

The Lord disciplines those He
loves, and He punishes
everyone He accepts as a son.

Hebrews 12:6

187.

You will never be the person you
can be if pressure, tension, and
discipline are taken out of your life.

James G. Bilkey

Communication

188.

Remember not only to say the right
thing in the right place, but far more
difficult still, to leave unsaid the
wrong thing at the tempting moment.

Benjamin Franklin

189.

The greatest problem in communication
is the illusion that it has been achieved.

190.

To shout, accuse and disparage is
seldom successful in an attempt to
change the behavior of people of any age.

Dr. James Dobson

191.

You have not converted a man
because you have silenced him.

John Morley

192.

It takes a great man to be a good listener.

Sir Arthur Helps

193.

Avoid letting temper block
progress – keep cool.

William Feather

194.

Good temper is an estate for life.

William Hazlitt

195.

Good temper, like a sunny day,
sheds a ray of brightness over
everything; it is the sweetener of toil
and the soother of disquietude!

Washington Irving

196.

Do not embitter your children,
or they will become discouraged.

Colossians 3:21

197.

Of all the things you wear, your expression is the most important.

Janet Lane

198.

Do not be quick with your mouth, do not be hasty in your heart.

Ecclesiastes 5:2

199.

Speak softly and sweetly. If your words are soft and sweet, they won't be as hard to swallow if you have to eat them.

200.

The test of good manners is to be able to put up pleasantly with bad ones.

Wendell Wilkie

201.

A torn jacket is soon mended, but hard words bruise the heart of a child.

Henry Wadsworth Longfellow

202.

Conquering the tongue is far better
than fasting on bread and water.

St. John of the Cross

203.

Don't laugh at a child's ambitions.
There is no sting as sharp as ridicule,
and laughter is often ridicule to a child.

Dale Carnegie

204.

When God wants to speak and
deal with us, He does not avail
Himself of an angel but of parents,
or the pastor, or of our neighbor.

Martin Luther

Success and Failure

205.

Four steps to achievement:
1. Plan purposefully
2. Prepare prayerfully
3. Proceed positively
4. Pursue persistently.

William A. Ward

206.

Yard by yard, all tasks are hard.
Inch by inch, they're all a cinch.

207.

Said will be a little ahead,
but *done* should follow at his heel.

Charles. H. Spurgeon

208.

Thou shalt ever joy at eventide
if you spend the day fruitfully.

Thomas à Kempis

209.

People rarely succeed unless they
have fun in what they are doing.

Dale Carnegie

210.

I long to accomplish a great
and noble task, but it is my chief duty
to accomplish small tasks
as if they were great and noble.

Helen Keller

211.

Every accomplishment
starts with the decision to try.

212.

It is more important to know where you
are going than to get there more quickly.
Do not mistake activity for achievement.

Mabel Newcomber

213.

Excuses are the nails used
to build a house of failure.

214.

Past failures are guidepost
to future successes.

215.

Men's best successes come
after their disappointments.

Henry Ward Beecher

216.

Failure is the opportunity to
begin again more intelligently.

Henry Ford

217.

Failure doesn't mean God has abandoned you; it does mean God has a better way.

218.

It is nobler to try something and fail than to try nothing and succeed. The result may be the same, but you won't be.

219.

I haven't failed, I've found 10 000 ways that don't work.

Thomas Edison

220.

There is no failure except in no longer trying.

Elbert Hubbard

Leadership and Character

221.

There is a great force
hidden in a gentle command.

George Herbert

222.

You must be careful how you walk,
and where you go, for there are those
following you who will set
their feet where yours are set.

Robert E. Lee

223.

I'd rather get ten men to do
the job than do the job of ten men.

Dwight L. Moody

224.

It is the part of a good shepherd
to shear his flock, not to skin it.

Latin Proverb

225.

Leadership is found in
becoming servant of all.

Richard Foster

226.

If you command wisely,
you'll be obeyed cheerfully.

Thomas Fuller

227.

"You have not cheated or oppressed
us," they replied. "You have not
taken anything from anyone's hand."

1 Samuel 12:4

228.

A man who wants to lead the
orchestra must turn his back on the crowd.

James Crook

229.

You do not lead people
by hitting them
over the head – that's
assault, not leadership.

Dwight D. Eisenhower

230.

Those who can command
themselves, can command others.

William Hazlitt

231.

The final test of a leader is that he
leaves behind him in other men
the conviction and the will to carry on.

Walter Lippmann

232.

Leadership is action, not position.

Donald H. McGannon

233.

The crux of leadership is that you
must constantly stop to consider
how your decisions will influence people.

Michigan State Police Maxim

234.

A great leader never sets
himself above his followers
except in carrying responsibilities.

Jules Ormont

235.

Trust is the emotional glue that
binds followers and leaders together.

Warren Bennis and Bert Nanus

236.

Even a child is known by his actions,
by whether his conduct is pure and right.

Proverbs 20:11

237.

He that has not served
knows not how to command.

Henry Wadsworth Longfellow

238.

Your real caliber is measured
by the consideration and
tolerance you have for others.

William J. H. Boetcker

239.

Character is a diamond
that scratches another stone.

Cyrus A. Bartol

240.

We often pray for purity, unselfishness,
for the highest qualities of character,
and forget that these things cannot
be given, but must be earned.

Lyman Abbott

241.

Good character is the quality which
makes one dependable whether being
watched or not, which makes one truthful
when it is to one's advantage to be a
little less than truthful.

Arthur S. Adams

242.

Courtesy, kindness, sincerity, truthfulness,
thoughtfulness, and good manners translated
into behavior reflect one's true character.

Henry F. Banks

243.

Character is formed, not by
laws, commands and decrees, but by
quiet influence, unconscious
suggestion and personal guidance.

Marion L. Burton

244.

You can easily judge the character of
others by how they treat those who
can do nothing for them or to them.

Malcolm Forbes

245.

People seldom improve if they have no
other model but themselves to copy after.

Oliver Goldsmith

246.

Character is not made in a crisis, only exhibited.

Robert Freeman

Prayer and Patience

247.

Seven days without
prayer makes one weak.

Allen E. Bartlett

248.

He who runs from God in
the morning will scarcely
find Him the rest of the day.

John Bunyan

249.

It is good for us to keep some
account of our prayers, that we
may not unsay them in our practice.

Matthew Henry

250.

Very early in the morning,
while it was still dark, Jesus got up,
left the house and went off
to a solitary place, where He prayed.

Mark 1:35

251.

Prayer is conversation with God.

Clement of Alexandria

252.

Prayer is a cry of hope.

French Proverb

253.

Our prayer and God's mercy are like
two buckets in a well; while the
one ascends the other descends.

Mark Hopkins

254.

Prayer is not merely an occasional
impulse to which we respond when we
are in trouble: prayer is a life attitude.

Walter A. Mueller

255.

More things are wrought by
prayer than this world dreams of.

Alfred Lord Tennyson

256.

Work as if you were to live 100 years,
pray as if you were to die tomorrow.

Benjamin Franklin

257.

"Where two or three come together
in My name, there am I with them."

Matthew 18:20

258.

Waiting is God's school,
wherein we learn some of His
most valuable lessons for us.

259.

Be patient with others as
God has been with you.

260.

Patience and perseverance have a
magical effect before which difficulties
disappear and obstacles vanish.

John Quincy Adams

261.

Patience is the companion of wisdom.

St. Augustine

262.

Where there is patience and humility,
there is neither anger nor vexation.

Francis of Assis

263.

True patience grows with the growth of love.

Gregory the Great

264.

The principal part of faith is patience.

George MacDonald

265.

Patience and diligence,
like faith, remove mountains.

William Penn

266.

Obedience is the fruit of faith;
patience the bloom of the fruit.

Christina Rossetti

267.

Endurance is patience concentrated.

Thomas Carlyle

268.

He is not truly patient who will endure only
as much as he pleases. A truly patient person
bears all, and it matters not whether he is
wronged by someone whose social standing
is superior, inferior, or equal to his own.

Thomas à Kempis

269.

He who waits on God never waits too long.

Chuck Wagner

270.

If you patiently accept what comes,
you will always pray with joy.

Evagrios the Solitary

271.

May I be patient! It is so difficult to make
real what one believes, and to make these
trials, as they are intended, real blessings.

John Henry Newman

272.

Patience with others is Love,
patience with self is Hope,
patience with God is Faith.

Adel Bestavros

Love and Kindness

273.

Kindness is more important than
wisdom, and the recognition
of this is the beginning of wisdom.

Theodore Isaac Rubin

274.

An anxious heart weighs a man
down, but a kind word cheers him up.

Proverbs 12:25

275.

A smile is the universal
language of kindness.

276.

The right kind of heart
is a kind heart like God's.

277.

You can't speak a kind word too soon, for
you never know how soon it will be too late.

278.

He who plants kindness gathers love.

St. Basil

279.

Do unto others even if
they never ever do unto you.

Mary Ellen Edmunds

280.

Kindness is the noblest
weapon to conquer with.

Thomas Fuller

281.

A kind heart is a fountain
of gladness, making everything
in its vicinity freshen into smiles.

Washington Irving

282.

If I can put one touch of rosy sunset
into the life of any man or woman,
I shall feel that I have worked with God.

John MacDonald

283.

Wherever there is a human being,
there is an opportunity for kindness.

Seneca

284.

Be the living expression of God's
kindness; kindness in your face, kindness
in your eyes, kindness in your smile,
kindness in your warm greeting.

Mother Teresa

285.

Kind words can be short and easy to
speak, but their echoes are truly endless.

Mother Teresa

286.

If you stop to be kind,
you must swerve
often from your path.

Mary Webb

287.

Love always seeks to help, never to hurt.

288.

The best portion
of a good man's life:
His little nameless,
unremembered acts
of kindness and love.

William Wordsworth

289.

The heart benevolent and
kind the most resembles God.

Robert Burns

290.

God's love is unconditional.
Be sure that yours is too.

291.

Love means loving the
unlovable – or it is no virtue at all.

292.

Do all the good you can
By all the means you can
In all the ways you can
In all the places you can
To all the people you can
As long as ever you can.

John Wesley

293.

He alone loves the Creator
perfectly who manifests
a pure love for his neighbor.

Venerable Bede

294.

God regards with how much
love a person performs a work,
rather than how much he does.

Thomas à Kempis

abcdef
ghijkl
mnopq
rstuv
wxyz

295.

To love is to will the good of another.

Thomas Aquinas

296.

Love is the beauty of the soul.

St. Augustine

297.

Love is the doorway through
which the human soul passes
from selfishness to service
and from solitude to
kinship with all mankind.

298.

In labors of love, every day is payday.

Gaines Brewster

299.

He does much who loves much.

Thomas à Kempis

300.

Love is the sum of all virtue,
and love disposes us to do good.

Jonathan Edwards

301.

Love has power to give in a moment
what toil can scarcely reach in an age.

Johann Wolfgang von Goethe

302.

The test of love
is in how one relates
not to saints and scholars,
but to rascals.

Abraham Joshua Heschel

303.

The soul that walks in love
neither tires others nor grows tired.

St. John of the Cross

304.

Love is the only fire
hot enough to melt the iron
obstinacy of a creature's will.

Alexander MacLaren

305.

Love me when I least deserve it,
because that's when I really need it.

Swedish Proverb

306.

We can do no great things;
only small things with great love.

Mother Teresa

307.

Love is a great teacher.

St. Augustine

Encouragement

308.

To ease one another's
heartache is to forget one's own.

Abraham Lincoln

309.

If you want to change people
without giving offense or arousing
resentment, use encouragement.

Dale Carnegie

310.

Those who are lifting the world
upward and onward are those
who encourage more than criticize.

Elizabeth Harrison

311.

A smile of encouragement
at the right moment may act like
sunlight on a closed flower; it may be
the turning point for a struggling life.

Alfred A. Montapert

312.

People have a way of becoming
what you encourage them to be –
not what you nag them to be.

Scudder N. Parker

313.

Shared joy is a double joy
and shared sorrow is a half-sorrow.

Swedish Proverb

314.

Encouragement is the oxygen of the soul.

315.

Patting a fellow on the back is
the best way to get a chip off his shoulder.

316.

Encouragement costs you nothing
to give, but it is priceless to receive.

317.

"What do you give a man
who has everything?" the pretty
teenager asked her mother.
"Encouragement, dear," she replied.

318.

I praise loudly, I blame softly.

Catherine II of Russia

319.

Encouragement after censure
is as the sun after a shower.

Johann Wolfgang von Goethe

320.

Expect people to be better than they
are; it helps them to become better.
But don't be disappointed when they
are not; it helps them to keep trying.

Merry Browne

Growth

321.

If you are pleased with what you are, you have stopped already. If you say, "it is enough," you are lost. Keep on walking, moving forward, trying for the goal. Don't try to stop on the way, or to go back, or to deviate from it.

St. Augustine

322.

We all want progress, but if you're on the wrong road, progress means doing an about-turn and walking back to the right road; in that case, the man who turns back soonest is the most progressive.

C. S. Lewis

323.

We want our children to grow up to be such persons that ill-fortune, if they meet with it, will bring out strength in them, and that good fortune will not trip them up but make them winners.

324.

Pygmies placed on
the shoulders of
giants see more than
the giants themselves.

Lucan

325.

Don't be yourself, be superior
to the fellow you were yesterday.

326.

He who limps is still walking.

Stanislaw J. Lec

327.

The head grows by taking in,
but the heart grows by giving out.

328.

We must always change,
renew, rejuvenate ourselves;
otherwise we harden.

Johann Wolfgang von Goethe

329.

Be not afraid of growing slowly,
be afraid of standing still.

Chinese Proverb

330.

If you think you're tops,
you won't do much climbing.

Arnold Glasgow

331.

The rung of a ladder was never
meant to rest upon, but only to
hold a man's foot long enough to enable
him to put the other somewhat higher.

Thomas H. Huxley

Worry

332.

Much that worries us beforehand
can afterwards, quite unexpectedly,
have a happy and simple solution.
Worries just don't matter. Things really
are in a better hand than ours.

Dietrich Bonhoeffer

333.

Never try to carry tomorrow's
burdens with today's grace.

334.

Worry does not empty tomorrow of its
sorrow; it empties today of its strength.

Corrie ten Boom

335.

Blessed is the man
who is too busy to worry
in the daytime and
too sleepy to worry at night.

336.

I believe God is managing affairs
and that He doesn't need any advice
from me. With God in charge, I believe
everything will work out for the best in
the end. So what is there to worry about?

Henry Ford

337.

It ain't no use putting up
your umbrella till it rains.

Alice Caldwell Rice

338.

In all trouble you should seek God.

St. Augustine

339.

Feed not your spirit on anything but
God. Cast off concern about things, and
bear peace and recollection in your heart.

St. John of the Cross

340.

Oh, how great peace and quietness
would he possess who should
cut off all vain anxiety and
place all confidence in God.

Thomas à Kempis

Faith

341.

Faith is to believe
what we do not see; and
the reward of this faith
is to see what we believe.

St. Augustine

342.

Faith never knows
where it is being led,
but it loves and knows
the One who is leading.

Oswald Chambers

343.

"If you have faith as small as a mustard
seed, you can say to this mountain,
'Move from here to there' and it will
move. Nothing will be impossible for you."

Matthew 17:20

344.

Faith goes up the stairs that love has made
and looks out the window that hope has opened.

Charles H. Spurgeon

345.

Faith is knowing there is an ocean
because you have seen a brook.

William Arthur Ward

346.

Faith is the reservoir from which
we draw power. It provides the extra
push that helps one to carry on.

Charles A. Anspach

347.

Faith that the thing can be done
is essential to any great achievement.

Thomas N. Carruthers

348.

There is many a thing which the
world calls disappointment, but there
is no such word in the dictionary of faith.

John Newton

Time

349.

The method of the enterprising
is to plan with audacity
and execute with vigor.

Christian Bovée

350.

The man who is prepared
has his battle half-fought.

Miguel de Cervantes

351.

Plan ahead. It wasn't
raining when Noah built the ark.

Richard Cushing

352.

By failing to prepare you
are preparing to fail.

Benjamin Franklin

353.

Time is a dressmaker
specializing in alterations.

Faith Baldwin

354.

Just because
something doesn't
do what you planned it to do
doesn't mean it is useless.

355.

You and I must not complain
if our plans break down,
if we have done our part.
That probably means
that the plans of the One
who knows more
than we do have succeeded.

Edward Everett Hale

356.

You will never "find" time for anything.
If you want time you must make it.

Charles Buxton

357.

Well arranged time is the
mark of a well arranged mind.

Pitman

358.

There is no such thing
as not enough time
if you're doing
what you want to do.

Robert Half

359.

Most time is wasted, not in hours,
but in minutes. A bucket with a small
hole in the bottom gets just as empty as
a bucket that is deliberately kicked over.

Paul J. Meyer

360.

It is familiarity with life that makes
time speed quickly. When every day is
a step into the unknown, as for children, the
days are long with gathering of experience.

George Gissing

361.

The man who wastes today lamenting yesterday
will waste tomorrow lamenting today.

Philip M. Raskin

362.

The best preparation for tomorrow
is to do today's work superbly well.

Sir William Osler

363.

We work not only to produce,
but to give value to time.

Eugène Delacroix

364.

Time is like money;
the less we have of it to spend,
the further we make it go.

Josh Billings

365.

Don't think of how you are
going to spend your time – use it.

Wilma Askinas